Moving Tides

Contents **Page**

written by Pam Holden

Red Rocket Readers™
Engineered by Flying Start Books

Tides are the rise and fall of the sea. High tide is when the water is deep and comes up high on the shore.

Low tide is when the water is shallow and does not come up as far.

Tides change when the moon and the sun pull on the oceans and make them rise.

High tides happen as the sea rises, and low tides happen as it falls. Most places have two high tides and two low tides each day.

Strong winds and storms make tides come up much higher than usual.

Sea walls have been built to stop damage from huge waves.

Tides are important for fishermen. There are charts to tell when high and low tides will happen.

Fishermen need to know the best times to move their boats and to catch fish.

Big ships need to move at high tide when the water is deeper.

It is safer to swim when the water is flowing in than when the tide is pulling out.

There are reefs and tide pools that are home to many sea animals and plants. Fish swim in with the tide to catch food.

Fishermen know that high tide is a good time to catch fish there.

At low tide, you can see the rocky tide pools. Some of us like to go to the shore at low tide to dig for food or shells in the sand.

Birds will hunt on the shore for food.

High tides bring clean water from the deep sea to keep places healthy and fresh – for the sea animals that live there, and for us to enjoy.